Christmas ~ good!

TRIXIE TREATS & HOLIDAY WISDOM

YORKVILLE PRESS
NEW YORK, NEW YORK

For information, contact Yorkville Press
1202 Lexington Avenue, #315, New York, N.Y. 10028.
www.yorkvillepress.com

DESIGN BY Tina Taylor, T2 Design
PHOTOGRAPHY BY Monique Stauder
ILLUSTRATIONS Copyright ©2005 by Janet Cleland

Library of Congress Cataloging-in-Publication Data
is on file with publisher.

ISBN 0-9767442-3-6
Printed in Canada by Friesens

jms 10 9 8 7 6 5 4 3 2 1

Christmas is Good!
TRIXIE TREATS & HOLIDAY WISDOM

By TRIXIE KOONTZ, dog
Edited by DEAN KOONTZ

Photography by Monique Stauder
Illustrations by Janet Cleland

CANINE COMPANIONS
FOR INDEPENDENCE

Introduction

I, Trixie Koontz (who is dog) was asked by publisher to write about Christmas. I like publisher. Nice lady. But I wrote one book already—Life is Good! Lessons in Joyful Living. One is more than Lassie ever wrote. (Rin Tin Tin wrote 800-page epic novel about Peloponnesian War but couldn't get published. Couldn't even get agent.) One is enough. Time to go sniffing for skunks in bushes, or something.

 Two reasons I say okay, publisher lady, will write book. First, royalties go to Canine Companions for Independence, fabulous organization trained me to be service dog. Money trains other dogs for disabled people. Second, Trixie (who is me) loves Christmas!

Love it, love it, love it!!! Yuletide carols being sung by choir! Silver bells! City sidewalks, busy sidewalks, dressed in holiday style! Halls decked, mistletoe hung! Folks dressed up like Eskimos! Jack Frost nipping your nose! Tiny tots with eyes aglow! No. Wait. Forget that last one. Tiny tots with eyes aglow reminds me of "Village of the Damned," scary movie. Saw it, hid under bed for two days.

Sometimes seems people forget wonder of Christmas. Dog like me could help people see wonder again. Dogs see wonder in everything. Tennis balls! Old shoe! Stupid rope tug toy! Dust ball! Hey, look, grass!!!!! Roll, roll, wriggle, eat, roll, wriggle, eat, spit up! That's just grass! Christmas has lots more better wonder stuff than grass!

Christmas has magic and love and
        reindeer with electrified noses,
                and miracles!. . . .

Come with me, Trixie, and see!

Things for Dogs
To Do at Christmas

Form group to sing carols.
People will yell Shut up and throw things.
Some things might be food.

Secretly squirm under Christmas dinner table.
Pass gas. Everyone will blame Grandpa.

*

Roll giant snowball down hill.
If timed to intersect passing cat,
could fill you with good cheer
for entire month.

Stupid laws don't allow dogs to drive cars.
But is no law against driving sleds and sleighs.

Say prayers.
Don't forget part about sausages.

Trixie's Tips to Dogs for a Happier Christmas

If caught being naughty, look cute. Always works.

*

Christmas Eve, Family will leave plate of cookies for Santa.
You eat cookies. Replace with celery sticks.
Santa will just think you have health-conscious family.

If elf in pointy hat tries to take your toys and treats,
claiming "Santa mistake," is not really elf.
Is disguised cat. Beware feline treachery.

Pretend to love stupid tug toy.
Later, when family asleep,
can play video game.

Lights on tree look like sugar-gum candy. They are not.
Don't bite. Candy canes are okay. Eat ten. Eat twenty.
Eat all candy canes. Don't worry if have to throw up.
Will be lots of empty gift boxes.

Give thanks to God for being dog.
He gave us the joy of angels.

Christmas is time for family
to come together and celebrate.
Even crazy Aunt Edna
should be welcome.

Trixie's Tips to People for a Happier Christmas

Make extra pumpkin pies. Dad loves 'em.
Remember when Dad ate two whole pies last Christmas Eve?
Yeah, it was Dad. Bad Dad. He had amnesia caused by
pumpkin overdose, but it was him. Could happen again.
Put on kitchen counter to cool.
Put near EDGE of kitchen counter.

Big fat cinnamon-scented Christmas candles smell
good. Taste okay. BUT DO NOT EAT.
Gastrointestinal calamity makes for
less happy holiday.

*

Sending handmade Christmas cards
is a good way to say "I'm thinking of you."
So is sending sausage.

*

Do not tie cat to tree for decoration.
Is funny, but not worth losing your nose.

*

If aluminum Christmas tree is so pretty,
why didn't God grow forests of them?
Think about it.

*

Turkey is suitable
Christmas-dinner entrée.
Farmer Earl's Mystery
Mammal Canned Stew is not.

Sharing love is more important than giving gifts.
But, how much can you really love me
if you don't give me anything? Think about it.

My Favorite Moments from Christmases Past

Eighteen wheeler loaded with frankfurters
skids off highway, crashes into our living room.

*

Cat next door gets whole truckload of
coal from Santa. Or from someone.

I, Trixie, who is dog, switch gift tags.
Dad gets squeaking plush-toy duck.
I get snowmobile.

Mom really likes slippers I crocheted for her
from my own hair. Makes me happy even though
I wind up with carpal-tunnel syndrome of the paw.

Mom puts miniature golden retriever in manger scene,
beside cradle. Later, I dream I was there 2,000 years ago,
on that night of hope and perfect peace.

People think Christmas is about gifts.
Is not about gifts. Is about Jesus,
love, hope and dog treats.

Christmas Secrets Revealed

Frosty the Snowman is not jolly soul.
Is foul-tempered grump intoxicated with celebrity.

*

Given his schedule, is not surprising but Santa Claus
has million-dollar-a-year Starbucks habit.

*

Mrs. Claus's first name is Bernice.
Her brother is Jack Frost. She wears
fur-lined orthopedic shoes. They smell nice.

*

Chestnuts roasting on open fires have
caused 1,236 serious holiday blazes.

*

Sometimes when Santa's behind on deliveries,
Easter Bunny helps out. But elves must follow him
to sweep up droppings.

Santa's sleigh is actually pulled by dogs.
Self-aggrandizing reindeer just have better publicity agent.

Santa's 5 Worst Christmas Crises

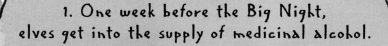

1. One week before the Big Night, elves get into the supply of medicinal alcohol.

*

2. Discovery that Rudolph's nose emits dangerous levels of radioactivity.

*

3. Temporary failure of antigravity device causes sleigh to plunge 20,000 feet. Reindeer traumatized. Santa returns to North Pole to change pants.

*

4. Thousands of little girls, still angry over previous year's shortage of Mary-Kate and Ashley dolls, are waiting for Santa with Wiffle bats and worse.

5. Three words: unionized elf workshop.

Trixie's Holiday Wish List

1. Sausages.
2. Sausages.
3. Sausages.
4. Sausages.
5. Peanut butter.
6. Sausages.
7. Potato chips.
8. Pretzels.
9. Meatballs.
10. Meatballs.
11. Sausage meatballs.
12. Peanut butter sausages.
13. Pepcid AC.
14. Seventy-eight tennis balls.
15. Twenty-five tennis balls.
16. Nine rubber balls.

17. DVD of "America's Funniest
Stupid-Cat videos!"

18. A partridge in a pear tree.

19. Bottle of Billy Joe Bob's partridge bar-bee-que hot sauce.

20. Sausage.

21. Tattoo of Garfield the cat on my butt.

22. World peace.

23. One hundred snappy comebacks for when mom and dad say "bad dog."

24. Psychological counseling for mentally disturbed little dog who thinks he saw cow jump over the moon and dish run away with spoon.

25. Scientific discovery that cats are sole cause of human aging.

26. Seven million pints of wild berry tofutti.

27. Driving lessons.

28. Map to Jimmy Dean sausage factory.

29. Map to Farmer John bacon factory.

30. Map to Ben & Jerry ice cream factory.

31. Liposuction as needed.

32. All fleas in hell.

33. Night vision cat scope.

34. Pepper spray to deal with aggressive mailmen.

35. Federal law against stupid yellow-vinyl dog raincoats.

36. Apology from Disney for stereotyping all dogs as dumb by creating and promoting witless character named Goofy.

37. Sausage.

Holiday Fun for Dogs and Their People

Play Frisbee in snow. If don't have snow,
play Frisbee anyway. If don't have Frisbee, throw cat.

*

Go out to nice restaurant. Order way too much food.
Bring leftovers home to dog.
Repeat all twelve days of Christmas.

*

Have snowball fight. No yellow snow!

*

Good dogs are not allowed to chase cars.
So you chase cars, give dog vicarious pleasure.

*

Craft homemade popcorn-ball tree ornaments.
Eat popcorn balls.

Read A Christmas Carol by Charles Dickens.
Discuss structure of metaphors and
symbolic purpose of supernatural entities
appearing in the narrative.

Take dog to nursing home. Pooch will cheer up
sad patients. Is the right Christmas spirit -
if you don't steal their slippers.

For me, Trixie, who is dog,
   Christmas is best time of year.
      Except for all the reindeer poop.

The Dark Side of Christmas

1. Snowman with scary-looking black coal teeth
whispers, "Gonna eat me a tasty dog."

2. Rawhide treat gets stuck in throat.
Emergency yuletide trip to vet.

*

3. Receive knitted dog sweater and booties,
forced to pose for humiliating pictures.

*

4. Psycho elf, Burt Gnarly.

*

5. Santa on sugar high from free cookies,
drives reindeer into side of
Goodyear blimp.

*

6. Yams.

Trixie's Hassle-Free Gift Guide for People

Is not necessary to spend fortune
on gift. If tastes like bacon,
everyone will like it.

PURRR-R-R-R

If gifts for family cat number more than
gifts for family dog, rethink your priorities.

*

If gifts for family dog are too many
to fit under tree, get bigger tree.

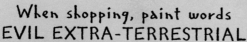

When shopping, paint words
EVIL EXTRA-TERRESTRIAL
on forehead. In even crowded stores, you will be
given plenty of elbow room, and clerks will wait on
you quick if you shout, "Want buy this now!"

*

If squeaks, is fun toy. If bounces, is fun toy.
If squeaks, bounces, and shouts "Cherry Mistmas,"
is Uncle Ned falling down stairs
after too much spiked egg nog.

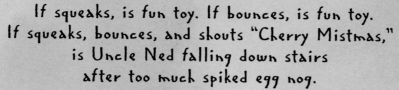

When store is sold out of hot item, scream at clerk,
snarl at customer who got last one in stock, stomp feet
and shriek. Then remember - when no room at the inn,
Mary and Joseph went to manger without complaint.
Now you feel mean, selfish, stupid. Learning humility is
first step to understanding true meaning of Christmas.

Christmas is not about getting.
Is about giving. So give me sausages!

Trixie's Holiday Favorites

Favorite Christmas treat:
The most recent one I ate.

*

Favorite Christmas moment:
When I get the next treat.

*

Favorite tree ornament:
Dog portrayed as angel. Is so true.

*

Favorite Christmas music:
CD titled "The Chipmunks Sing Handel's Messiah."

*

Favorite Christmas movie:
Die Hard.

*

Favorite Christmas activity:
Three-dimensional chess.

Favorite way to end Christmas Day:
Say prayers, then open eyes and see God smiling.
Dogs see God. Being able to see Him
is His gift to the innocent.

I'm dreaming of a white Christmas.
Turkey breast, mashed potato,
sugar cookies, vanilla ice cream . . .

Trixie Says You Know You Have the Right Christmas Spirit if...

oops!

You can't resist wearing
nifty fake antlers to work.

You Know You Have the Right Christmas Spirit if:
You make Christmas wreath for dog.
Out of frankfurters.

*

You give car-jacker money for dinner
and movie before he drives off in your car.

*

Grandma feels sorry for turkey, cooks fried tofu
instead - and it's all right with you!

*

Visions of sugar plums dance in your head.
(If make you nauseous, might not be
Christmas spirit. Might be bad sushi.)

The mere sight of those you love brings happy tears to your eyes, and you remember to thank God for your life, and theirs.

Queenie

Cooper

Rover

Brutus

Duke

Fifi

I, Trixie (who is dog) would like to thank all my dog friends who appeared in this book (even though they're not real) Rocky, Zoe, Duke, Brutus, Queenie, Cooper, Rover, Fifi, Sybll, and a reluctant thanks to Beast, the cat.

Special thanks to all my real dog friends at Canine Companions for Independence for all the good work you do!

Zoe

Sybll

Rocky

Beast

Christmas is Good!